This book belongs to

_____

Stevie Wonder

By Mary Nhin

This book is dedicated to my children - Mikey, Kobe, and Jojo.

Copyright © 2023 by Grow Grit Press LLC. All rights reserved. No part of this book may be reproduced in any form without permission in writing from the publisher. Please send bulk order requests to growgritpress@gmail.com
Paperback ISBN: 978-1-63731-824-9 Hardcover ISBN: 978-1-63731-826-3
Printed and bound in the USA. MiniMovers.tv

Hi, I'm Stevie Wonder.

I was born prematurely and the third of my parents' five children.

I was sent to the NICU and received too much oxygen therapy. As a result, my retinas became detached, leaving me blind.

This is how I saw the world.

Life wasn't easy for me, but I had a dream to be a world famous music artist.

When I was younger, my good friend, John, and I played on street corners and at parties. I enjoyed playing several instruments including the harmonica, piano, and drums.

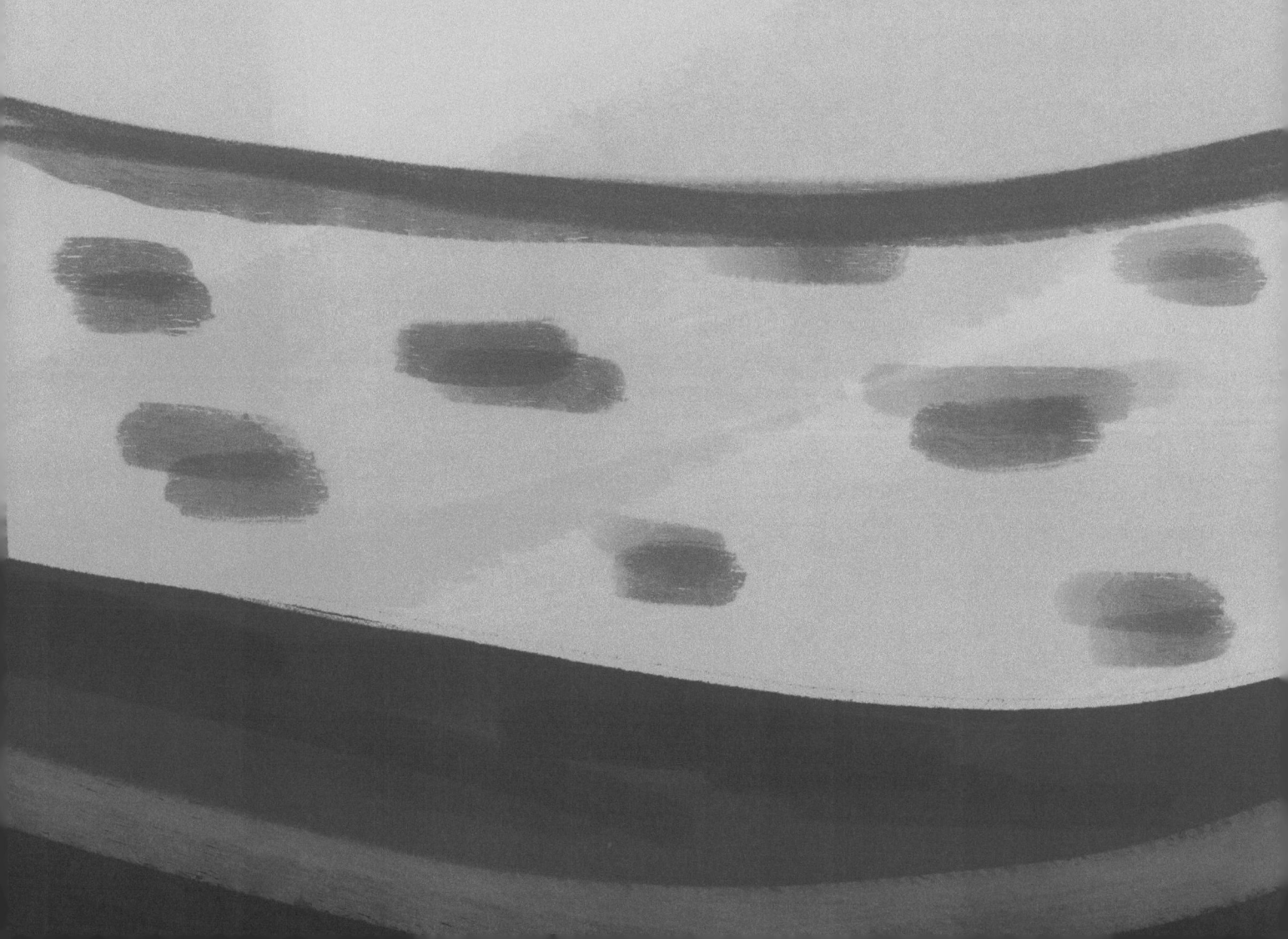

When I was eleven years old, I was discovered by Mr. White, who gave me a five year contract. We received a check each week and I was provided a tutor to strengthen my skills as an artist while on tour. This is when I received the professional name Little Stevie Wonder.

At first, my music was not successful, but I kept trying my best!

Finally, at thirteen years old, I was the youngest artist to make it to the top of the charts with my hit single "Fingertips".

As I got older, my voice changed and my record label thought about canceling me. Just when I was about to be canceled, Berry Gordy, my producer, persuaded the record label to keep me.

When I got older, I dropped the "little" from my professional name so that I was just known as Stevie Wonder.

I came out with popular love songs such as "I Was Made to Love Her" and more top hits.

At 25 years old, I won two consecutive Grammys! I also got to meet a lot of inspiring artists and play with them, such as the Beatles.

I made history by winning three Grammys in one year!

I was the first to have a number one hit song the day it was released, staying at the top of the chart for 14 weeks straight.

"I want to thank Stevie Wonder for not releasing an album this year."

One year, I didn't release an album, but I still won Grammys!

Most of my songs are written about my own life and experiences. I think that's what people love about my music most; my music contains my feelings so they have a lot of soul in them.

On my 35th birthday, I was honored by the United Nations Special Committee Against Apartheid for standing up against racism.

I've helped raise money for charity events, releasing over 100 million albums worldwide, and I've won 25 Grammys!

Just because a man lacks the use of his eyes doesn't mean he lacks vision.

Timeline

1963 - Stevie becomes the youngest to hit top charts

1976 - Stevie wins most Grammys in one year

1980 - Stevie campaigns for MLK day as a federal holiday

1999 - Stevie receives an honorary doctorate in Fine Arts from Rutgers University

minimovers.tv

 @marynhin   @GrowGrit
#minimoversandshakers

 Mary Nhin   Ninja Life Hacks

 Ninja Life Hacks

 @ninjalifehacks.tv

www.ingramcontent.com/pod-product-compliance
Lightning Source LLC
Chambersburg PA
CBHW041523070526
44585CB00002B/63